Rx

poems

JOSH SAPAN

Red Hen Press | *Pasadena, CA*

Book design by Mark E. Cull
Layout assistance by Isiah Lyons

Library of Congress Cataloging-in-Publication Data

Names: Sapan, Joshua, author.
Title: Rx: poems / Josh Sapan.
Description: First edition. | Pasadena, CA: Red Hen Press, [2023]
Identifiers: LCCN 2022026224 (print) | LCCN 2022026225 (ebook) | ISBN
  9781636280394 (hardcover) | ISBN 9781636280400 (ebook)
Subjects: LCGFT: Poetry.
Classification: LCC PS3619.A628 R9 2023 (print) | LCC PS3619.A628 (ebook)
  | DDC 811/.6—dc23/eng/20220606
LC record available at https://lccn.loc.gov/2022026224
LC ebook record available at https://lccn.loc.gov/2022026225

The National Endowment for the Arts, the Los Angeles County Arts Commission, the Ahmanson Foundation, the Dwight Stuart Youth Fund, the Max Factor Family Foundation, the Pasadena Tournament of Roses Foundation, the Pasadena Arts & Culture Commission and the City of Pasadena Cultural Affairs Division, the City of Los Angeles Department of Cultural Affairs, the Audrey & Sydney Irmas Charitable Foundation, the Meta & George Rosenberg Foundation, the Albert and Elaine Borchard Foundation, the Adams Family Foundation, Amazon Literary Partnership, the Sam Francis Foundation, and the Mara W. Breech Foundation partially support Red Hen Press.

First Edition
Published by Red Hen Press
www.redhen.org

To Nate and Claire
There's no poem that can say how happy you've made me.

Contents

Night Quiet   11

Delaware, December   12

Here in the Midwest   13

The Crows   14

Nine Months, Three Days   15

Morning   18

Davis Creek   20

Sixty Days Since the Solstice   21

Blue Moon Wisteria   22

Dr. Lodge   23

Inside   24

Ten Minutes to Sioux City   25

In Spain   27

Holiday at Home '72   28

Solstice   29

Holiday   30

Jim   31

Chopin's Heart   32

The Marriott   33

Papa Max   34

Houseplant   35

Last Night   36

Your Straw Hat   37

Fantasy of a History   38

Dorothy and the Stars   39

Shortcake and Scooter   41

Walk in the Dark   43

Winter   44

Watergap   45

Friend   46

Tree Trimmer   47

Tessa Sapan   48

My Brother Garth   49

A Grateful List   51

The Day Porter   52

℞

Night Quiet

The wind pauses
to listen
to night quiet
glancing inside windows
where large screens
out of earshot
glow like silent films.

The wind kneels
praying to the moon
for the earth
to spin faster
so invisible molecules
fall into the large black hole
where demons are sent.

Delaware, December

The river froze that night.
Mountainous chunks of ice
grinding against one another,
a large animal in distress.

Chipmunks burrowed
beneath driftwood up
at the eddy.
Bears blinked awake.

The moon wondered
then slipped away
behind a night cloud.
Morning broke.

The sun reflected
floating diamonds
on granite riverbank
stirring everyone awake.

Here in the Midwest

Here in the Midwest,
spaces take up the room.
They rule the future;
giant powerful ghosts.

The whole country
is afraid of Wisconsin.
It is either
flown over
driven through at night
hidden out in the open.

When a stranger
moves to Fond Du Lac
he learns not to stand
in the shadows.

The Crows

The crows are back
in the black walnut,
the sawtooth oak,
the sugar maple.

Clustering
close to the clouds
drowning the sounds
of the red throated loons
keeping the
white throated owl
quiet.

Avoiding
the pitch pine
and all beach plums.

This March
they came
to stay
maybe
forever.

Nine Months, Three Days

You move
molecules of air
with care
carrying
the fragile cake
you baked
for Wade.

You call him
on his black
rotary phone
fifteen feet
from our front door
close to heaven.
It gives his knees
hope they will move again.
His hands believe they will steady
his heart
that it will pump forever.
He tells you
the story
of his father
Tifton,
a mischievous man.

Milton disappeared from his job
after thirty-five years
taking orders

for five good tomatoes,
seedless grapes
and sometimes lamb.
He typed a letter to you
when you found him.
He was embarrassed
by his bad English
He listens to Mozart,
loves his grandchildren
vows you were his
nicest customer.

Zeppo
whimpers
when you close
the front door.
He hears
your steps
on the bricks
when you return,
shimmies
in a dance.

Now nine months and three days in,
the crows gone south,
the big white moon
slips
to the other side
of the planet.
The growing hedge
exhales.

The radio
plays
a world
far away.
No one knocks
at the door.
The lights
in the houses
across the harbor
turn off.
The space
between us
narrows
so I am
always close
to you.

Morning

Dew invades the cut lawn
arriving silently
in clouds that drape
the grass like a tarp.

Crickets
march slowly over the lawn
moving in a perfect battle line
from porch to pool.

Hard skulls,
beady eyes.
Some cousins,
some brothers.

Near the driveway,
one cricket stops next to a rock,
his legs fly up in an epileptic grip.
He dreamed of dying at a pond at an old age.

The cricket lines meet
then there's only one
string of black
separating into small pieces.

It sounds like a page
being crumpled.
Backs are snapped
legs cracked, heads squashed.

The lawn is clean, combed, manicured.
Another day begins
in the washed-out yellow light
of early dawn.

Davis Creek

Davis Creek in back of our house
is prettiest at its lowest point
when the sea grass stands tall.
Egrets admire it
like their own well-tended garden.

Today shows
the next step of the seventy-three-year-old woman
and the twenty-seven-month-old boy filled with surprise
at seeing a rabbit's eyes
holding statue still on the steps

Today the school of minnows
take their longest swim.
From the creek to Peconic Bay,
they dive deep to rest
then pause to listen
to the quiet breathing of clams.

Today the sand crab winks
to say
that soon he builds a hard shell,
that protects the tender skin.

Today knows time is long
like this cedar tree
with its big trunk of memory.
Today is a day to see the admired cloud
over Peconic Bay descend gently to the ground

Sixty Days Since the Solstice

Forgotten fans rotate
over summer porches.
Valentine's Day cards
wilt in racks
at the pharmacy.
Oystercatchers
hide behind brown marsh grass.
The lights are only on in back
of Mallory's house
on Chequit Street.

But the white winged scoters
are gliding in wind drafts.
Piping plovers have mated.
Daylight reflects on ground snow
to altostratus clouds.

The winter solstice
was sixty days ago.
Now eyelids flutter
in the morning
anticipating long days.
The sand too hot
for a toddler's touch
to bake the last
bit of infection away.

Blue Moon Wisteria

Sea grass turns brown
then green.
The swing
on the big tree dips left.

If I stay
through several Septembers
the reporter
will write

Attended PS 187
watched the magic of
the expressway
expand forever east.

Played stickball
in the parking lot.
No church
No nickname

Just the sweet sounds
of Ann, Claire & Nate
climbing the stairs
blue moon wisteria.

Dr. Lodge

Harry's shirt was distracted from his trousers.
Blue and white oxford stripes
sailing free in a ten-knot wind
around the office.
Everyone felt a good tack
in the waiting room.

Harry was a new kind of superman.
Just Clark Kent:
no glasses, no costumes.

For hundreds of us
he was a healer, teacher, friend.
Preaching test results
as matters of love.
He worked on our veins,
          kept eyes on our souls.

Inside

The planet turns
suspiciously
glancing up, down, around
looking for scarlet
on clouds,
specks on the moon
in the mirror.

Inside with you
it is the blue green
of early May
where Shelter Island Sound
meets sky, wind
sends thousands of little waves
cleansing the world.

Ten Minutes to Sioux City

Ten minutes to Sioux City
there's cotton on the land.
Watch the world for dinner,
hold a peach in my hand.

A South Dakota lady
drops herself in the aisle
like a book falling
from a brown bag.

The war, the war
that burned
children's bodies,
all I had was tea!

Her eyes glow
like shiny marbles
she watches highway lights
like stars.

Below on the plain
a handsome man
sells machines
talking like a television.

Caught up in lawnmowers.
He would like to dance naked
downtown at the Remo
with Chota.

Rhoda the teenager tells me
she flies first class all the way
runs patterns around her parents
leaping to fame.

She sighs, heaves her breasts
exhales like ocean spray.
"I can sew up any tear hole or
person that gets in my way."

I hear a baby's scream
my thoughts move faster than sound.
They resound in the clouds
like a lost child in a baseball stadium.

In Spain

The evening lies down easily.
Proud men carry
one arm at their side
in shadows.

The woman begins walking home
hawking tickets for the lottery game
"Quatro cinco menos seis"
"Quatro cinco menos seis"

Then smell of rabbit
brings the night out
like a dancing funeral
limbs losing control.

Sailors brush the avenues
carrying glory in their boots.
They inhabit the bars like mosquitoes
playing games with oranges and stories.

The children asleep,
the grown-ups accounted for.
Down the snake streets lost in a maze
comes an odd harmony . . .

"Do you believe in God"
"We believe in God"
"Do you believe in God"
          "We believe in God"

Holiday at Home '72

Crocodile chatter
floats in endless circles
around the mature water crescents.

My eyes
never close
under water.
It is said
in the most dangerous
fish pools
I have a stare
    like my father.

Solstice

Ah, the moment
an exhale
carries away
thoughts
that won't rest.

The shortest day
is the first day
of renewal.

Holiday

All the creatures agree
not to speak,
not a whisper
not a sound
after Thanksgiving's last gasp.

The highways settle,
the sidewalks empty
getting ready
for the footsteps
from out of town.

The subway stops
giving the granite a break
from holding up skyscrapers
that stand straight in the sky
never glancing down.

The East River flows
up and around,
the tidal estuary
never hurrying
its pattern.

A puppy detects
a sign of new life
invisible but joyous.
The first gift
    of holidays.

Jim

He kept a pocket full of pills,
didn't count the glasses of scotch
while he sailed big boats.

Was friendly with stars,
borrowing small meteors
to spin into sky,
shining boomerangs
returning to the delight of all.

Jim held wind in his hand
as the sun took a slow arc
without a shadow.

He walked in deck shoes made of sympathy,
counseled strangers
turning their demons
into small droplets
that evaporated forever.

Chopin's Heart

I scatter my mother's ashes
next to Holy Cross Chapel in Warsaw

Where Chopin's heart bobs in time
with his Nocturne No. 2 in a jar of formaldehyde.

June afternoon trees cast wide shadows.
Yellow freesia resists evening.

Can't keep my eyes off a young woman who refuses
to abandon her boyfriend's lap.

I hold my mother's ashes high.
A bit of wind carries them, passing the second-floor window.

Past Chopin's heart, then another window
     then the steeple, then they're gone.

The Marriott

Smiles at the desk,
concierge standing by
The walls and floors
swept, vacuumed and shined
A rest from oneself.

Glide down
to the Washington and Lincoln ballrooms
for a celebration of a birth
or seventy-five years.

Ride toward the sky
and the Club.
Buffet changes at
7, noon, then 5.

Room 1506
next door
a key free click
to a private life
for a night.

Papa Max

Are you quiet
curled in a coffin, papa?

Some atheist box
far away from
the salt breeze,
the tap of the foot on the boardwalk,
the neon from Coney Island,
the endless sound of your own voice.

Your words were
your gospel,
Yiddish and English
in the same sentence,
philosophy and religion
in the same breath.

What nonsense
your bald head made
stiff and red
supported
by your cane
on top of the world.

Houseplant

I bought a speckled houseplant
to lean toward the light
each day when we wake
for the few dusty sunrays
that creep in over the rooftops.

Time
its wilting leaves yellowing,
its shape still beautiful.
When it turns brown and brittle
I won't throw it out

Hoping a new season
will make it green again.

Last Night

You were too fast to see.
Only remembered
in blurred pictures.

Made my body
begin to move
without will.

Then you were gone,
leaving only the smell of jealousy
that stifles the dance.

But for one fluid arm
whose flickering fingers
seemed to gently touch my wrist.

Your Straw Hat

On the foot bridge over the creek
the sand mounds separate
by a quiet incoming tide.
A salty breeze
rides above
breathing life
into tall grass
with invisible bubbles of oxygen.

Our mothers said goodbye
leaving a thick paged book of notes, menus and stories
on the nightstand.
Their willful genes
permanently in the capillaries
of their grandchildren,
securing their futures
with centuries of the past.

Today I hear the serenade
of the ceremony,
the winds whooshing
like a stage whisper
carrying your straw hat and my dreams
over the bay.
In a gust it sends them
        to the sky forever.

Fantasy of a History

You try to fire me
from life
with the glare from your glasses
when I preach
the virtues of disbelief
three times
in three different ways.

In sum
you say a guru
created
the thoughts you think
2000 years ago
sitting in a circle
outdoors.

If I were there
with him
and his profound beard
maybe we would
roll over in the grass
look at each other
differently.

Dorothy and the Stars

Dorothy the majorette
had fun
married young.

Her silver baton
which once swept the stars
hung behind her gown in the closet.

Once—
in the middle
of a thought.

Cooking in the kitchen,
Dorothy began a split.
Her feet slid coolly apart.

Her fingers began to swan,
curl,
twist.

She watched
her breasts
float up.

The ground came closer.
The stars on the wall
began to dance.

Leaping sideways—
backwards & forwards
spreading sparkling trailers in their path.

Shortcake and Scooter

This night
we quietly call Canada
reflects its bright shivers
between our eyes
like the light from the fenders
of the two Chevys
sitting in the lot.

We wait watching the window
occasionally shifting couch cushions
that sound
like grandfather sighing.
Yesterday I named you Faith in my dog talk;
you called me handsome
in your bird whistle.

Being Sunday
we sat in the sun all afternoon
only inches
above the black asphalt
with white stripes
counting every car containing
a family.

In the evening,
we watched the sun descend
behind the ring of stores
thinking what we could have
if we wanted anything.

You wanted shortcake
me a scooter.

Walk in the Dark

We walk in the dark
lighting candles, listening to the transistor radio,
bumping into furniture.
Pauses between words long.
I can't tell where anyone is standing:
whether they have moved;
if someone is lost.

This year of hurricanes, floods, wars
like a tale from the Bible.
The planet hotter,
spinning faster,
shifting on its axis?
The floor slopes down.

I hear the door open
Saturday morning.
You carry toasted bagels with cream cheese,
muffins with blueberries and cranberries.
Love so big,
it comes in a gigantic red box.
Everything I ever dreamed of.

Winter

December
is an early curtain
to colored glass illuminating
streets, bridges and buildings
that makes winter
bring myths to life.

Watergap

Flatrock lies underfoot,
a red November
hangs on the trees
of Callicoon mountain.

Once a boy from Aunt Lila's camp
pulled the shade down
and touched you
in the glass gazebo by the stream.

Your mother walks on the wooden footbridge
that passes the dam frogs die in.
They float on their backs
with white bloated bellies.

The Chinese caretaker comes once a week
scoops them up for the bonsai garden.
"About that boy" she says putting her hands
in your pockets.

You feel her clenched fists.

Friend

I put you in my pocket
like loose change.

I try not to squeeze
your nose

or scratch your eyes
when I reach for you

On Sundays
or in dreams.

You look at me
like your camp counselor

or your cousin
and talk

Like a carefree friend
sipping coffee.

Tree Trimmer

In 1969 Nils threw a casual Molotov cocktail
into Krogers' grocery store
to object to the Vietnam War
two years in the Dane County Jail.

He liked to close his eyes
listen to the roar of the crowd
from the Badgers football game
two blocks away.

Nils was unusual
for the son of a surgeon.
Chose to trim trees
a hundred feet closer to heaven.

Hoping to stay
high above the ground forever,
Taught me to be superman
for a minute.

I never knew anyone
who played so casually
with weapons
and his mind.

Nils wore his manhood
in a tidy way
beneath an ascot
        of delight.

Tessa Sapan

You suck your final
blue-fog medicine breath
from the nebulizer:
alien spaceship with a broken carburetor.

Twist your eyes
in your shrunken
Jewish voodoo-master skull
sending a hex
on the Clorox doctors
who treat heartbreak with Haldol.

You are the saddest,
maddest and thinnest
in your frozen emphysema frame.
You are more sister, mother and motherfucker.

Your cousins were hidden from Hitler.
Your uncles and aunts
gassed in camps.
You were listener, watcher, lover,
drinker, dancer, actor,
writer, cook and mother.

You kiss us goodbye
with a smile
that transplants your soul
        into ours without blood or stitches.

My Brother Garth

My brother Garth
was gentle in Queens,
when kids were tough.
Loose in Great Neck,
when kids were tight.

My brother Garth
was my protector.
Dumbbells, curls, sit ups, bench presses,
he made good on becoming a man of iron;
always stuck up for me.

My brother Garth wrote hundreds of songs.
Pulled me into his room the first time
"I want to hold your hand"
was on the radio.
He told me the world had changed.

My brother Garth believed
in Dylan Thomas,
Bob Dylan and John Lennon.
Believed he should attend twelfth grade
the minimum number of days required by law.

My brother Garth was called by
George Washington University
to negotiate between
black students and the school
in the student strike of 1968.

My brother Garth
wandered the streets.
Called me Sir.
My brother Garth was a schizophrenic.
So dear, so gone.

A Grateful List

The bridge
The song
Your mother and father
The maid of honor
Your hat
The wind

My mother
Scat singing
Tap dancing
The vows
The movie
The wind

The best man
Our daughter
Waiting
Twenty six years
The wind
Carrying you
To me.

The Day Porter

John McGowan walked the halls
like a giant secret saint,
wisps of grey hair, wide smile and strong arms
wrapping you in a hug.

His large hands clasped behind your back
lifting you off the ground
for a moment of gravityless joy
in busy hallways.

He seemed sent from heaven
to place a private mirror
to us in white shirts and ties
so we could see more clearly.

John McGowan got off the bus
on his way home
in November's early winter darkness
covered by his blue uniform.

He lay down on a small piece of Brooklyn concrete
to watch the earth turn gently towards tomorrow
when an invisible piece of his spirit broke off
to grow in everyone he touched.

Biographical Note

Josh Sapan is a longtime television and film executive. Despite that, his poems have appeared in a number of literary publications.